QUICK & EASY
PIZZAS

QUICK & EASY
PIZZAS

Shirley Gill

Photography by Karl Adamson

HERMES
HOUSE

This edition published by Hermes House
27 West 20th Street, New York, NY 10011

HERMES HOUSE books are available for bulk purchase for sales promotion
and for premium use. For details, write or call the sales director,
Hermes House, 27 West 20th Street, New York, NY 10011;
(800) 354-9657

Hermes House is an imprint of
Anness Publishing Inc.

ISBN 1-84038-350-X

Publisher: Joanna Lorenz
Series Editor: Joanne Rippin
Designer: Peter Laws
Photographer: Karl Adamson

Printed and bound in China

© Anness Publishing Limited 1998
Updated © 1999
1 3 5 7 9 10 8 6 4 2

CONTENTS

INTRODUCTION

The pizza originated as a cheap, savory snack in Naples, sold from street stalls or in special eating houses, but it has long since been upgraded to a universally popular main meal. Today's favorite fast food, pizzas are quick and filling meals for people in a hurry. However, if you take the time to make your own you will find they are easy and fun – the simplest are often the best, provided the ingredients are fresh and flavorful. They are suitable for all tastes, with toppings that have become far more generous and varied than the traditional Italian pizzas.

In this book you will find instructions on how to make basic pizza dough as well as several delicious alternatives. The amount of dough needed for one recipe is small and very easy to handle, and preparations are simple and straightforward. If using readymade bases, these recipes can be made in less than one hour.

A word on baking pizzas: the very best results are achieved by cooking them in a traditional brick oven to make them light and crisp. Even without a brick oven, the home cook can achieve excellent results with a pizza stone and it is well worth buying one if you make pizzas frequently. The direct heat makes them wonderfully crisp. Pizzas must be eaten hot straight from the oven as they soon harden in an unappetizing way.

Pizzas need not be served just as snacks or main meals; they can become stylish starters, when they are made as small pizzettes or served in thin wedges. They also make great party food – a festive array of pizzas will please any crowd!

This is a collection for pizza lovers everywhere. Although most of the recipes contain cheese, this can be reduced if you desire a lighter pizza. There is also a final section of interesting Italian breads, full of great flavors and textures just waiting to be tasted.

Herbs and Spices

Herbs and spices are essential for seasoning pizzas and improving their flavor. Fresh herbs should be used whenever possible. Buy growing herbs in pots: this not only ensures the herbs are as fresh as possible, but also provides a continuous supply.

Basil (sweet basil)
Intensely aromatic, basil has a distinctive peppery flavor. The leaves can be used to garnish pizzas and are also ideal with tomato in a summer salad; chopped or shredded it can become the main seasoning ingredient.

Black peppercorns
Black peppercorns are best used freshly ground in a mill or crushed as the taste and aroma disappears quickly.

Chilies (fresh and dried chili products)
Fresh chilies vary in taste, from mild to fiery hot. Generally the large, round fleshy varieties are milder than the small, thin-skinned pointed ones. For a milder, spicy flavor, remove the seeds and veins.

Red chili flakes are made from dried, crushed chilies and are somewhat milder than fresh chilies. They can be heated with olive oil to make chili oil for brushing over pizza bases or used to add bite to pizza toppings and fillings for calzone.

Mild chili powder is a commercially prepared mixture of chili, ground herbs and spices. It can be used to flavor more contemporary-styled pizzas.

Chives
A member of the onion family, the long, narrow green leaves are best used as a garnish or chopped and added to the pizza dough for extra flavor.

Cilantro
The delicate light green leaves have an unusual flavor and distinctive aroma. Chopped leaves are often used in combination with chilies, especially in Californian-style pizzas. The fresh leaves also make an attractive garnish.

Cumin
These seeds have a warm, earthy flavor and aromatic fragrance and are sold whole or ground. Use in pizzas, especially those with chili and oregano, for a Mexican flavor.

Curly parsley
This provides color and gives a fresh flavor to pizza toppings.

Italian parsley
This variety has much more flavor than common curly parsley, but they can be used interchangeably.

Herbes de Provence
A dried herb mixture of thyme, savory, rosemary, marjoram and oregano. It is especially good mixed with black olives and added to pizza doughs or sprinkled on top before cooking.

Nutmeg
Nutmeg has a sweetish, highly aromatic flavor which has an affinity for rich foods. It is used to great effect in stuffed pizzas and pizza toppings, especially those containing spinach.

Oregano
An aromatic and highly flavored herb. Oregano features strongly in Italian cooking, where it is sprinkled on to pizzas.

Rosemary
Rosemary, with its dark piney, tarry aroma, can be overpowering, but when used judiciously, it can add a delicious flavor to vegetables like potatoes for an unusual pizza topping.

Saffron
The dried stigmas of the saffron crocus, saffron is the most expensive spice in the world, but fortunately very little is needed in most recipes, sometimes as little as a pinch. Pungent and brilliantly yellow colored, saffron is available as strands or ground.

Sage
Just a few leaves can deliciously flavor a pizza topping, especially with a rich-tasting cheese like Gorgonzola; sage tends to overpower subtle flavors.

Salt
Salt balances the action of yeast and is an integral part of bread-making. For seasoning, use sea salt flakes or refined table salt; the former has a slightly stronger flavor so use it sparingly.

Thyme
This is excellent chopped or crumbled, and stirred into tomato sauce or sprinkled on to pizzas. Whole sprigs can be used as a garnish.

saffron

red chili flakes

cilantro

mild chili powder

fresh red chilies

chives

thyme

curly parsley

Italian parsley

ground cumin

herbes de Provence

nutmeg

sage

rosemary

oregano

basil

black peppercorns

sea salt

Fresh Vegetables for Pizzas

Never has vegetable cooking been so exciting. A quick glance in the greengrocers and supermarkets reveals a remarkable choice. There are baby eggplant, wild mushrooms, red onions, colorful peppers, hot-tasting chilies, as well as fennel and wonderful asparagus – a truly international offering, providing endless possibilities to the cook.

As vegetables are so full of color they make attractive and tempting pizza toppings. Choose the best quality fresh vegetables for maximum flavor and scout around to see what is newly in season. Get to know which of them should be pre-cooked – mushrooms, zucchini and eggplant for example – and which can be used raw – onions, leek and tomato slices. Vegetable pizzas are not just for vegetarians; they are for everyone who enjoys exciting food, inventively prepared and presented with style.

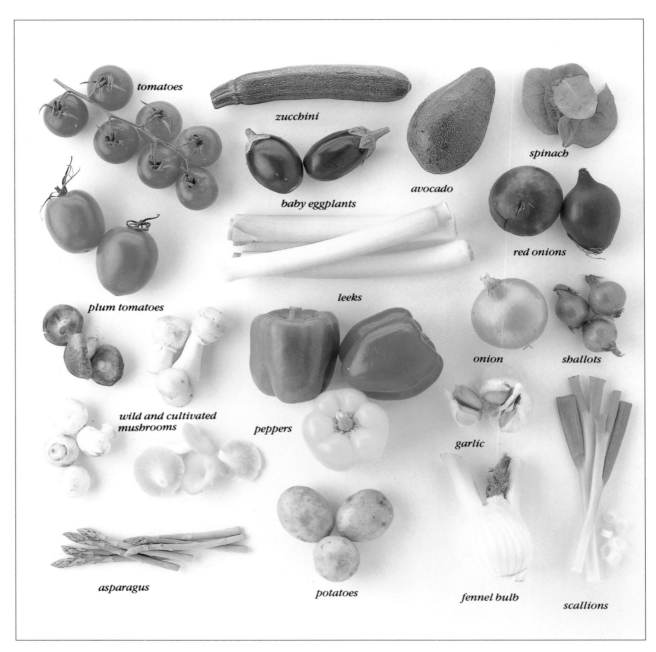

tomatoes

zucchini

avocado

spinach

baby eggplants

red onions

plum tomatoes

leeks

onion

shallots

wild and cultivated mushrooms

peppers

garlic

asparagus

potatoes

fennel bulb

scallions

Meat and Fish for Pizzas

Pizzas with a meat or fish topping make a marvelous substantial lunch or supper dish served with tossed salad leaves. They can be topped with a wealth of delicious ingredients. Sliced cured meats, salamis, ham and sausages are perennial favorites. Look for them in supermarkets where they may be either prepacked in the meat section or at the delicatessen counter. Chicken and ground beef can also be used in highly imaginative ways.

Fresh fish and shellfish also make tempting pizza toppings. Favorites such as shrimp, mussels, squid and salmon may be used alone or mixed for a good variety of flavors. Canned fish such as tuna and anchovies are also an important feature of pizza toppings. If you find anchovies too salty, it helps to soak them in milk before use. For best results, some shellfish are added halfway through the cooking time to ensure that they are not overcooked. When you are shopping for fish and shellfish the most important quality to look for is freshness.

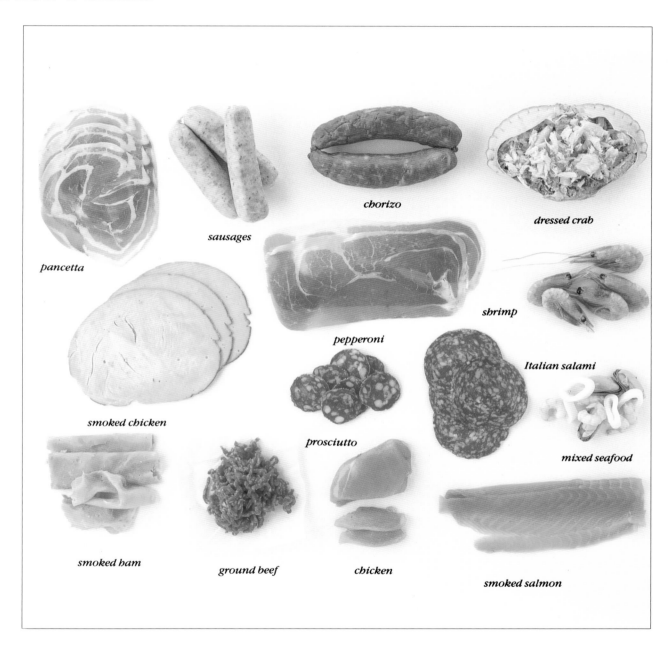

pancetta

sausages

chorizo

dressed crab

smoked chicken

shrimp

pepperoni

Italian salami

prosciutto

mixed seafood

smoked ham

ground beef

chicken

smoked salmon

Pantry Cupboard

For the most part the recipes in this book call upon fresh everyday ingredients and certain essential items from the pantry cupboard. There are a few special ingredients, however, which are worth hunting for. They may seem expensive, but just a little will go a long way to give your pizzas character and flair.

Anchovies
Canned anchovies imported from the Mediterranean have been filleted and salted before being packed in oil. They are an important flavoring ingredient and garnish for many pizzas.

Artichoke hearts
When these are specified in a recipe, those packed in oil in jars have been used. They are ideal for pizza toppings.

Capers
These are the flower buds of a shrub native to the Mediterranean which are preserved in vinegar and salt or salt alone. They have a strong piquant flavor and should be used with care.

Cornmeal (polenta)
Adds texture and an earthy flavour to the basic pizza dough.

Flour
White flour contains 72–74 per cent of the wheat grain. It is available in strong, plain and self-rising forms.

Traditional pizza bases are made from bread dough, which is usually made with unbleached all-purpose flour. Some white flours are also bleached, so look for "unbleached" on the label for untreated flour.

Bread flour is used to make focaccia, a flattish bread with various toppings.

Self-rising white flour has had leavening or raising agents added to it, and is suitable for a scone pizza base.

Whole wheat flour is simply flour milled from the whole grain with nothing added or taken away. Plain and self-rising whole wheat flours are used for making pizza doughs. You will find mixing it with white flour produces a dough lighter in color and texture. If you can find hard-wheat (durum) flour use it to make a beautiful golden pizza dough.

Olives
Green olives are unripe; black are fully ripe and have more flavor. They are widely available in many forms – whole or pitted, or stuffed with ingredients like pimientoes or anchovy fillets. You can buy them preserved in brine or oil, and they are used only in their preserved state. Pitted olives can be baked into bread or used as a garnish.

Olive oil
A "pure" olive oil of good quality is indispensable for making traditional Italian pizzas. Olive oil brushed on the dough and a drizzle over the topping offers flavor and also protection in the fierce heat of the oven. Ingredients such as garlic and chilies can be added to the oil to provide extra flavor. Extra virgin olive oil is usually a darker green and has a more intense flavor.

Pimiento
Pimiento is the Spanish word for pepper. The red variety is available packed whole into cans. Sweet flavored, with a bright red color, they are a useful pantry standby.

Pine nuts
These small, oval, creamy colored nuts with a sweet flavor are much appreciated in the Mediterranean and Middle East. They may be sprinkled on to pizzas to add texture, or used in sauces such as pesto, which can be spread over the dough base for extra flavor.

Rapid-rise dried yeast
Much faster and quicker to use than fresh or dried yeast, as its name implies. It does not need to be reconstituted in liquid first; but is mixed directly with the flour. Use lukewarm liquid to mix the dough as extreme temperatures can kill the yeast and the dough will not rise.

Red pesto
A richly aromatic sauce combining pesto with sun-dried tomatoes. Delicious on pizzas or stirred into sauces.

Sun-dried tomato paste
This has a richer, more intense flavor than ordinary tomato paste and makes a quick pizza topping. It also enriches sauces and gives a lovely color.

Tapenade
This is made from green or black olives ground to a paste with a little olive oil and seasoning. Delicious spread on to pizza bases or spooned on top just before serving, it is especially good with pizzas containing goat cheese.

Tomatoes: canned
No pantry cupboard should be without them! Canned tomatoes come either whole or crushed, ready for use in sauces and toppings.

Tomatoes: sun-dried in oil
Sun-dried tomatoes have a concentrated, salty flavor, which is excellent used in small quantities in breads and as a pizza topping.

Tomato paste
Useful for adding color, intensity and flavor to home-made tomato sauce.

Tuna
Canned tunafish is usually packed in oil, brine or water. It firm texture makes it a useful pizza topping.

Walnuts
Walnuts are excellent added to bread to serve with antipasti.

anchovies

pimiento

walnuts

olive oil

sun-dried tomatoes

tuna

pine nuts

canned tomatoes

sun-dried tomato paste

artichoke hearts

capers

cornmeal

tomato paste

red pesto

lack olives

green olives

rapid-rise dried yeast

plain flour

lack olive tapenade

green olive tapenade

whole wheat flour

bread flour

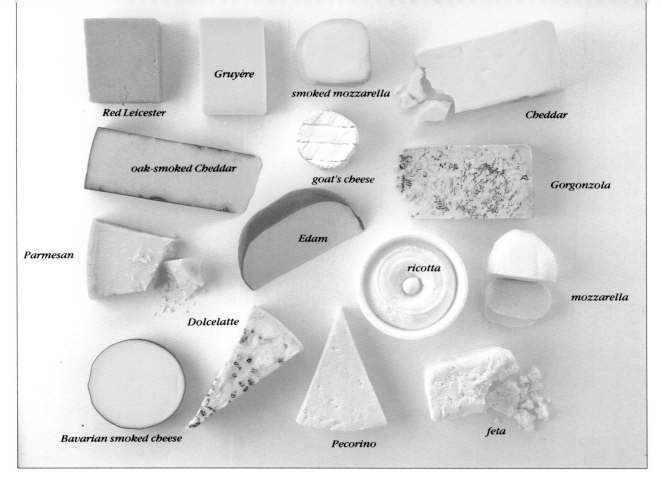

Gruyère
smoked mozzarella
Red Leicester
Cheddar
oak-smoked Cheddar
goat's cheese
Gorgonzola
Parmesan
Edam
ricotta
mozzarella
Dolcelatte
Bavarian smoked cheese
Pecorino
feta

Pizza Cheeses

One of the most important elements in the making of a tasty pizza is the cheese. Mozzarella is the cheese most often associated with pizza, but a variety of cheeses can be used, so experiment with different ones to suit your taste.

Cheddar
This cow's milk cheese is produced commercially but also by small dairy farmers, who make delicious varieties. Flavors can vary from mild to quite strong. It is a very versatile cheese, and ideal for cooking.

Edam
A Dutch ball-shaped cheese, firm and smooth in texture with a mild, nutty flavor.

Feta
Feta is a fairly hard cheese that crumbles easily on to pizzas. It is preserved in brine which accounts for its salty flavor. Rinse before using.

Goats cheese
Goats cheeses are small, generally shaped in logs, rounds, pyramids or ovals, and range in flavor from fresh and creamy to strong and tangy.

They cook well and are especially good with roasted vegetables for a tasty vegetarian pizza.

Gorgonzola *piccante*
This cheese is pleasantly sharp in flavor, with a spreadable texture and blue-green veins.

Gruyère
A hard cheese with a distinctive sweet and nutty taste, it is widely used in cooking as a good melting cheese.

Mozzarella
This versatile cheese is used in many pizza recipes for its astounding melting quality. Good mozzarella should be very white, fairly elastic and moist when cut.

Parmesan
Italy's most famous hard cheese, which is usually grated for cooking and serving with pizza. Always buy fresh Parmesan if you can, as it is by far the best.

Pecorino
An Italian sheep's cheese which has a fairly strong distinctive flavor. It is used in the same way as Parmesan.

Red Leicester
This cheese has a mild flavour and bright color.

Ricotta
A soft Italian whey cheese with a delicate, smooth flavor. It is ideal for use in fillings for calzone and panzerotti.

Saga Blue
A blue-veined, semi-soft cheese. It has a smooth, creamy texture and delicate piquant flavour.

Smoked Cheddar
A Cheddar variant which is excellent grated over pizzas, adding a distinctive flavor.

Smoked Gouda
Sold in rounds with a brown wax coating, this cheese has a pale creamy color and mild, smoky flavor with a smooth, soft texture.

Smoked mozzarella
Smoked mozzarella has a creamy, smoky taste that gives it a more distinctive flavor than the plain variety. It also has excellent melting properties.

Equipment

To make pizzas successfully you do not have to have special tools, but tasks are made simpler with the aid of certain utensils and gadgets.

Baking sheet
Choose a large heavy baking sheet that will not warp at high temperatures.

Chef's knife
This has a heavy, wide blade ideal for chopping.

Flour dredger
A useful piece of equipment for dusting the work surface.

Garlic press
This is a small metal gadget used for crushing garlic.

Grater
A multi-surfaced grater can be used for all grating purposes.

Jelly-roll pan
A rectangular tin, ideal for making hearty farmhouse pizzas.

Measuring cup
Essential for measuring liquid, these cups are available in a wide range of sizes.

Measuring spoons
Used for accurately measuring small amounts of ingredients.

Metal spoons
The best metal spoons are oval with a pointed end.

Mixing bowls
A set of bowls in various sizes is essential when cooking.

Nutmeg grater
This is a miniature grater used for grating whole nutmegs.

Rolling pin
Choose a long, heavy pin for even rolling.

Salt and pepper mills
These are used specifically for grinding coarse sea salt and whole peppercorns.

Olive oil can
Usually made of metal, it has a long, thin spout for drizzling oil on to pizzas.

Olive pitter
This removes stones from olives with one quick press.

Paring knife
A small knife for trimming and peeling vegetables.

Parmesan grater
A special grater for Parmesan.

Pastry brush
This is useful for brushing on oil, water or beaten egg white.

Pastry cutter
This is used for stamping out dough rounds.

Pizza stone
A terracotta round, used instead of a baking sheet or pizza pan. The stone absorbs and retains heat, and crisps the dough.

Pizza cutter/lifter
A dual-purpose gadget for cutting and serving pizzas.

Pizza pan
Traditional pizza pans are round and shallow. Deep-dish pizza pans are also available, but a square cake pan may be used instead. A perforated pizza pan allows steam to escape and encourages a crisp base.

Pizza wheel
This large cutting wheel is useful for easy slicing.

Wooden spoons
Essential in all kitchens is a set of wooden spoons.

Basic Pizza Dough

This simple bread base is rolled out thinly for a traditional pizza recipe.

MAKES
1 × 10–12 in round pizza
   base
4 × 5 in round pizza bases
1 × 12 × 7 in oblong pizza
   base

INGREDIENTS
1½ cups bread flour
¼ tsp salt
1 tsp rapid-rise dried yeast
½–⅔ cups lukewarm water
1 tbsp olive oil

1 Sift the flour and salt into a large mixing bowl.

2 Stir in the yeast.

3 Make a well in the center of the dry ingredients. Pour in the water and oil and mix with a spoon to a soft dough.

4 Knead the dough on a lightly floured surface for about 10 minutes until smooth and elastic.

5 Place the dough in a greased bowl and cover with plastic wrap. Let rise in a warm place for about 1 hour or until the dough has doubled in size.

6 Punch down the dough. Turn on to a lightly floured surface and knead again for 2–3 minutes. Roll out as required and place on a greased baking sheet. Pinch up the dough to make a rim. The dough is now ready for topping.

Deep-dish Pizza Dough

This recipe produces a deep and spongy base.

MAKES
1 × 10 in deep-dish pizza base

INGREDIENTS
2 cups bread flour
½ tsp salt
1 tsp rapid-rise dried yeast
⅔ cup lukewarm water
2 tbsp olive oil

Follow the method for Basic Pizza Dough. When the dough has doubled in size, punch down and knead for 2–3 minutes. Roll out the dough to fit a greased 10 in deep-dish pizza pan or square cake pan. Let the dough prove for 10 minutes, then add the topping. Alternatively, shape and place on a greased baking sheet.

Whole Wheat Pizza Dough

INGREDIENTS
3 oz/¾ cup whole wheat flour
¾ cup bread flour
¼ tsp salt
1 tsp rapid-rise dried yeast
½–⅔ cup lukewarm water
1 tbsp olive oil

Follow the method for Basic Pizza Dough. You may have to add a little extra water to form a soft dough, depending on the absorbency of the flour.

Cornmeal Pizza Dough

INGREDIENTS
1½ cups bread flour
¼ cup cornmeal
¼ tsp salt
1 tsp rapid-rise dried yeast
½–⅔ cup lukewarm water
1 tbsp olive oil

Follow the method for Basic Pizza Dough.

Scone Pizza Dough

The joy of using a scone mixture is it's quick to make and uses pantry cupboard ingredients.

MAKES
1 × 10 in round pizza base
1 × 12 × 7 in oblong pizza
　　base

INGREDIENTS
1 cup self-rising flour
1 cup self-rising whole wheat
　　flour
pinch of salt
4 tbsp butter, diced
⅔ cup milk

1 Mix together the flours and salt in a mixing bowl. Rub in the butter until the mixture resembles fine bread crumbs.

2 Add the milk and mix with a wooden spoon to a soft dough.

3 Knead lightly on a lightly floured surface until smooth. The dough is now ready to use.

Superquick Pizza Dough

If you're really pressed for time, try a packaged pizza dough mix. For best results roll out the dough to a 10–12 in circle; this is slightly larger than stated on the package, but it does produce a perfect thin, crispy base. For a deep-dish version use two packets.

ALSO MAKES
4 × 5 in round pizza bases
1 × 12 × 7 in oblong pizza
　　base

INGREDIENTS
1 × 5 oz package pizza base mix
½ cup lukewarm water

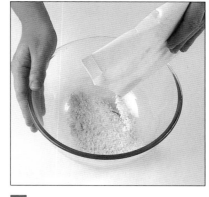

1 Empty the contents of the package into a mixing bowl.

2 Pour in the water and mix with a wooden spoon to a soft dough.

3 Turn the dough on to a lightly floured surface and knead for 5 minutes until smooth and elastic. The dough is now ready to use.

Using a Food Processor

For speed make the pizza dough in a food processor; let the machine do the mixing and kneading, then let the dough proof until doubled in size.

1 Put the flour, salt and yeast into a food processor. Process to mix for a few seconds.

2 Measure the water into a bowl and add the oil. With the machine running, add the liquid and process until the dough forms a soft ball. Leave to rest for 2 minutes, then process for 1 minute more to knead the dough.

3 Remove the dough from the processor and shape into a neat round. Place in a greased bowl and cover with plastic wrap. Let rise in a warm place for about 1 hour until doubled in size. Punch down and knead the dough for 2–3 minutes. The dough is now ready to use.

Readymade Pizza Bases

Fortunately for the busy cook it is now possible to buy fresh, frozen or long-life pizza bases from most supermarkets. Many are enriched with additional ingredients like cheese, herbs and onions. Although they never seem to taste as good as a real homemade pizza base they can be very useful to keep on hand. All you have to do is add your chosen topping and bake in the usual way.

Pitting Olives

Using a pitter is the easiest way to remove the pit from an olive, but you can also use a sharp knife.

1 Put the olive in the pitter, pointed end uppermost.

2 Squeeze the handles together to extract the pit.

Chopping Herbs

Use this method to chop herbs until they are as coarse or fine as you wish.

1 Strip the leaves from the stem and pile them on a cutting board.

2 Using a sharp knife cut the herbs into small pieces, holding the tip of the blade against the board and rocking the blade back and forth.

Tomato Sauce

Tomato sauce forms the basis of the topping in many of the recipes. Make sure it is well seasoned and thick before spreading it over the base. It will keep fresh in a covered container in the fridge for up to 3 days.

COVERS
1 × 10–12 in round pizza
   base
1 × 12 × 7 in oblong pizza
   base

INGREDIENTS
1 tbsp olive oil
1 onion, finely chopped
1 garlic clove, crushed
1 × 14 oz can chopped tomatoes
1 tbsp tomato paste
1 tbsp chopped fresh mixed herbs,
   such as parsley, thyme, basil and
   oregano
pinch of sugar
salt and black pepper

1 Heat the oil in a pan, add the onion and garlic and gently sauté for about 5 minutes until softened.

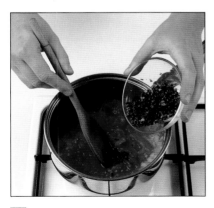

2 Add the tomatoes, tomato paste, herbs, sugar and seasoning.

3 Simmer, uncovered, stirring occasionally for 15–20 minutes or until the tomatoes have reduced to a thick pulp. Leave to cool.

Flavored Oils

For extra flavor brush these over the pizza base before adding the topping. They also form a kind of protective seal that keeps the crust crisp and dry.

CHILI

INGREDIENTS
⅔ cup olive oil
2 tsp tomato paste
1 tbsp dried red chili flakes

1 Heat the oil in a pan until very hot but not smoking. Stir in the tomato paste and red chili flakes. Leave to cool.

2 Pour the chili oil into a small jar or bottle. Cover and store in the fridge for up to one week.

GARLIC

INGREDIENTS
3–4 whole garlic cloves
½ cup olive oil

1 Peel the garlic cloves and put them into a small jar or bottle.

2 Pour in the oil, cover and refrigerate for up to 1 week.

Margherita

(Tomato, Basil and Mozzarella)
This classic pizza is simple to prepare. The sweet flavour of sun-ripened tomatoes works wonderfully with the basil and mozzarella.

Serves 2–3

INGREDIENTS
1 pizza base, about 10–12 in
　diameter
2 tbsp olive oil
1 quantity Tomato Sauce
5 oz mozzarella
2 ripe tomatoes, thinly sliced
6–8 fresh basil leaves
2 tbsp freshly grated Parmesan
black pepper

basil

mozzarella

Parmesan

olive oil

tomatoes

Tomato Sauce

1 Preheat the oven to 425°F. Brush the pizza base with 1 tbsp of the oil and then spread over the Tomato Sauce.

2 Cut the mozzarella into thin slices.

3 Arrange the sliced mozzarella and tomatoes on top of the pizza base.

4 Roughly tear the basil leaves, add and sprinkle with the Parmesan. Drizzle over the remaining oil and season with black pepper. Bake for 15–20 minutes until crisp and golden. Serve immediately.

Marinara

(Tomato and Garlic)

The combination of garlic, good quality olive oil and oregano give this pizza an unmistakably Italian flavor.

Serves 2–3

INGREDIENTS
4 tbsp olive oil
1½ lb plum tomatoes, peeled, seeded
  and chopped
1 pizza base, about 10–12 in
  diameter
4 garlic cloves, cut into slivers
1 tbsp chopped fresh oregano
salt and black pepper

olive oil

oregano

plum tomatoes

garlic

1 Preheat the oven to 425°F. Heat 2 tbsp of the oil in a pan. Add the tomatoes and cook, stirring frequently for about 5 minutes until soft.

2 Place the tomatoes in a strainer and leave to drain for about 5 minutes.

3 Transfer the tomatoes to a food processor or blender and purée until smooth.

4 Brush the pizza base with half the remaining oil. Spoon over the tomatoes and sprinkle with garlic and oregano. Drizzle over the remaining oil and season. Bake for 15–20 minutes until crisp and golden. Serve immediately.

Quattro Stagioni

(Four Seasons)
This traditional pizza is divided into quarters, each with a different topping to depict the four seasons of the year.

Serves 2–4

INGREDIENTS
3 tbsp olive oil
2 oz mushrooms, sliced
1 pizza base, about 10–12 in
   diameter
1 quantity Tomato Sauce
2 oz prosciutto
6 pitted black olives, chopped
4 bottled artichoke hearts in oil,
   drained
3 canned anchovy fillets, drained
2 oz mozzarella, thinly sliced
8 fresh basil leaves, shredded
black pepper

artichoke hearts

mozzarella

olive oil

Tomato Sauce

prosciutto

basil

mushrooms

black olives

anchovy fillets

1 Preheat the oven to 425°F. Heat 1 tbsp of the oil in a frying pan and fry the mushrooms until all the juices have evaporated. Leave to cool.

2 Brush the pizza base with half the remaining oil. Spread over the Tomato Sauce and mark into four equal sections with a knife.

3 Arrange the mushrooms over one section of the pizza.

4 Cut the prosciutto into strips and arrange with the olives on another section.

5 Thinly slice the artichoke hearts and arrange over a third section. Halve the anchovies lengthwise and arrange with the mozzarella over the fourth section.

6 Sprinkle the basil over. Drizzle the remaining oil over and season with black pepper. Bake for 15–20 minutes until crisp and golden. Serve immediately.

Napoletana

(Tomato, Mozzarella and Anchovies)
This pizza is a speciality of Naples. It is both one of the
simplest to prepare and the most tasty.

Serves 2–3

INGREDIENTS
1 pizza base, about 10–12 in
    diameter
2 tbsp olive oil
6 plum tomatoes
2 garlic cloves, chopped
4 oz mozzarella, grated
2 oz can anchovy fillets, drained and
    chopped
1 tbsp chopped fresh oregano
2 tbsp freshly grated Parmesan
black pepper

Parmesan

mozzarella

anchovy fillets

olive oil

plum tomatoes

garlic

oregano

1 Preheat the oven to 425°F. Brush the
pizza base with 1 tbsp of the oil. Put the
tomatoes in a bowl and pour over boiling
water. Leave for 30 seconds, then plunge
into cold water.

2 Peel, seed and coarsely chop the
tomatoes. Spoon the tomatoes over the
pizza base and sprinkle over the garlic.

3 Mix the mozzarella with the
anchovies and sprinkle over.

4 Sprinkle over the oregano and
Parmesan. Drizzle over the remaining oil
and season with black pepper. Bake for
15–20 minutes until crisp and golden.
Serve immediately.

Quattro Formaggi

(Four Cheeses)

Rich and tasty, these individual pizzas are quick to assemble, and the aroma of melting cheese is irresistible.

Serves 4

INGREDIENTS

1 quantity Basic or Superquick Pizza Dough
1 tbsp Garlic Oil
½ small red onion, very thinly sliced
2 oz Saga Blue
2 oz mozzarella
2 oz Gruyère, grated
2 tbsp freshly grated Parmesan
1 tbsp chopped fresh thyme
black pepper

red onion

mozzarella

Parmesan

Garlic Oil

Saga Blue

Gruyère

thyme

1 Preheat the oven to 425°F. Divide the dough into four pieces and roll out each one on a lightly floured surface into a 5 in circle. Place well apart on two greased baking sheets, then pinch up the dough edges to make a thin rim. Brush with Garlic Oil and top with the red onion.

2 Cut the Saga Blue and mozzarella into cubes and scatter over the bases.

3 Mix together the Gruyère, Parmesan and thyme and sprinkle over.

4 Grind over plenty of black pepper. Bake for 15–20 minutes until crisp and golden and the cheese is bubbling. Serve immediately.

Fiorentina

Spinach is the star ingredient of this pizza. A grating of nutmeg to heighten its flavor gives this pizza its unique character.

Serves 2–3

INGREDIENTS
6 oz fresh spinach
3 tbsp olive oil
1 small red onion, thinly sliced
1 pizza base, about 10–12 in
    diameter
1 quantity Tomato Sauce
freshly grated nutmeg
5 oz mozzarella
1 large egg
1 oz Gruyère, grated

mozzarella

Gruyère

Tomato Sauce

spinach

red onion

nutmeg

egg

1 Preheat the oven to 425°F. Remove the stems from the spinach and wash the leaves in plenty of cold water. Drain well and pat dry with paper towels.

2 Heat 1 tbsp of the oil and fry the onion until soft. Add the spinach and continue to fry until just wilted. Drain off any excess liquid.

3 Brush the pizza base with half the remaining oil. Spread over the Tomato Sauce, then top with the spinach mixture. Grate some nutmeg over.

4 Thinly slice the mozzarella and arrange over the spinach. Drizzle the remaining oil over. Bake for 10 minutes, then remove from the oven.

5 Make a small well in the center and drop the egg into the hole.

6 Sprinkle over the Gruyère and return to the oven for a further 5–10 minutes until crisp and golden. Serve immediately.

American Hot

This popular pizza is spiced with green chilies and pepperoni.

Serves 2–3

INGREDIENTS
1 pizza base, about 10–12 in
    diameter
1 tbsp olive oil
4 oz can peeled and chopped green
    chilies in brine, drained
1 quantity Tomato Sauce
3 oz sliced pepperoni
6 pitted black olives
1 tbsp chopped fresh oregano
4 oz mozzarella, grated
oregano leaves, to garnish

mozzarella

oregano

Tomato Sauce

pepperoni

olive oil

green chillies

black olives

1 Preheat the oven to 425°F. Brush the pizza base with the oil.

2 Stir the chilies into the sauce, and spread over the base.

3 Sprinkle the pepperoni over.

4 Halve the olives lengthwise and sprinkle over, with the oregano.

5 Sprinkle the grated mozzarella over and bake for 15–20 minutes until the pizza is crisp and golden.

VARIATION

You can make this pizza as hot as you like. For a really fiery version use fresh red or green chilies, cut into thin slices, in place of the chilies in brine.

6 Garnish with oregano leaves and serve immediately.

Prosciutto, Mushroom and Artichoke

Here is a pizza full of rich and varied flavors. For a delicious variation use mixed cultivated mushrooms.

Serves 2–3

INGREDIENTS
1 bunch scallions
4 tbsp olive oil
8 oz mushrooms, sliced
2 garlic cloves, chopped
1 pizza base, about 10–12 in
    diameter
8 slices prosciutto
4 bottled artichoke hearts in oil,
    drained and sliced
4 tbsp freshly grated Parmesan
salt and black pepper
thyme sprigs, to garnish

scallions

Parmesan

mushrooms

prosciutto

olive oil

artichoke hearts

1 Preheat the oven to 425°F. Trim the scallions, then chop all the white and some of the green stems.

2 Heat 2 tbsp of the oil in a frying pan. Add the scallions, mushrooms and garlic and fry over a moderate heat until all the juices have evaporated. Season and let cool.

3 Brush the pizza base with half the remaining oil. Arrange the prosciutto, mushrooms and artichoke hearts on top.

4 Sprinkle the Parmesan over, then drizzle the remaining oil over and season. Bake for 15–20 minutes. Garnish with thyme sprigs and serve immediately.

Chorizo and Corn

The combination of spicy chorizo and sweet, tender corn works well in this hearty and colorful pizza. For a simple variation you could use chopped fresh basil instead of Italian parsley.

Serves 2–3

INGREDIENTS

1 pizza base, about 10–12 in
    diameter
1 tbsp Garlic Oil
1 quantity Tomato Sauce
6 oz chorizo sausages
6 oz (drained weight) canned corn
    kernels
2 tbsp chopped fresh Italian
    parsley
2 oz mozzarella, grated
2 tbsp freshly grated Parmesan

Tomato Sauce

mozzarella

Italian parsley

Garlic Oil

chorizo sausages

Parmesan

sweetcorn

1 Preheat the oven to 425°F. Brush the pizza base with Garlic Oil and spread over the Tomato Sauce.

2 Skin and cut the chorizo sausages into chunks and scatter over the Tomato Sauce. Bake for 10 minutes then remove from the oven.

3 Sprinkle over the corn and Italian parsley.

4 Mix together the mozzarella and Parmesan and sprinkle over. Bake for a further 5–10 minutes until crisp and golden. Serve immediately.

Beef Chili

Ground beef, red kidney beans and smoky cheese combined with oregano, cumin and chilies give this pizza a Mexican character.

Serves 4

INGREDIENTS
2 tbsp olive oil
1 red onion, finely chopped
1 garlic clove, crushed
½ red bell pepper, seeded and finely chopped
6 oz lean ground beef
½ tsp ground cumin
2 fresh red chilies, seeded and chopped
4 oz (drained weight) canned red kidney beans
1 quantity Cornmeal Pizza Dough
1 quantity Tomato Sauce
1 tbsp chopped fresh oregano
2 oz mozzarella, grated
3 oz smoked Cheddar, grated
salt and black pepper

Tomato Sauce

red onion

ground beef

mozzarella

smoked Cheddar

red chilies

oregano

olive oil

red kidney beans

red bell peppers

1 Preheat the oven to 425°F. Heat 1 tbsp of the oil in a frying pan, add the onion, garlic and pepper and gently fry until soft. Increase the heat, add the beef and brown well, stirring constantly.

2 Add the cumin and chilies and continue to cook, stirring, for about 5 minutes. Add the beans and seasoning.

3 Roll out the dough on a surface dusted with cornmeal and use to line a 12 × 7 in greased jelly roll pan. Pinch up the dough edges to make a rim.

4 Spread the Tomato Sauce over.

5 Spoon the beef mixture over then sprinkle the oregano over.

6 Sprinkle the cheeses over and bake for 15–20 minutes until crisp and golden. Serve immediately.

VARIATION

If you prefer a milder version of this spicy pizza, reduce the amount of fresh chilies or leave them out altogether.

Chicken, Shiitake Mushroom and Cilantro

The addition of shiitake mushrooms adds an earthy flavor to this colorful pizza, while fresh red chili provides a hint of spiciness.

Serves 3–4

INGREDIENTS
3 tbsp olive oil
12 oz chicken breast fillets, skinned and cut into thin strips
1 bunch scallions, sliced
1 fresh red chili, seeded and chopped
1 red bell pepper, seeded and cut into thin strips
3 oz fresh shiitake mushrooms, wiped and sliced
3–4 tbsp chopped fresh cilantro
1 pizza base, about 10–12 in diameter
1 tbsp Chili Oil
5 oz mozzarella
salt and black pepper

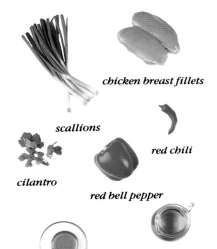

chicken breast fillets

scallions

red chili

cilantro

red bell pepper

olive oil

Chili Oil

shiitake mushrooms

1 Preheat the oven to 425°F. Heat 2 tbsp of the olive oil in a wok or large frying pan. Add the chicken, scallions, chili, pepper and mushrooms and stir-fry over a high heat for 2–3 minutes until the chicken is firm but still slightly pink within. Season to taste.

2 Pour off any excess oil, then set aside the chicken mixture to cool.

3 Stir the fresh cilantro into the chicken mixture.

4 Brush the pizza base with the chili oil.

5 Spoon the chicken mixture over and drizzle the remaining olive oil over.

6 Grate the mozzarella and sprinkle over. Bake for 15–20 minutes until crisp and golden. Serve immediately.

Pancetta, Leek and Smoked Mozzarella

Smoked mozzarella with its brownish smoky-flavored skin, pancetta and leeks make this an extremely tasty and easy-to-prepare pizza, ideal for a light lunch.

Serves 4

INGREDIENTS
2 tbsp freshly grated Parmesan
1 quantity Basic or Superquick Pizza
    Dough
2 tbsp olive oil
2 medium leeks
8–12 slices pancetta
5 oz smoked mozzarella
black pepper

pancetta

leeks

smoked mozzarella

olive oil

Parmesan

1 Preheat the oven to 425°F. Dust the work surface with the Parmesan, then knead into the dough. Divide the dough into four pieces and roll out each one to a 5 in circle. Place well apart on two greased baking sheets, then pinch up the edges to make a thin rim. Brush with 1 tbsp of the oil.

2 Trim and thinly slice the leeks.

3 Arrange the pancetta and leeks on the pizza bases.

4 Grate the smoked mozzarella and sprinkle over. Drizzle the remaining oil over and season with black pepper. Bake for 15–20 minutes until crisp and golden. Serve immediately.

Ham and Mozzarella Calzone

A calzone is a kind of "inside-out" pizza – the dough is on the outside and the filling on the inside. For a vegetarian version replace the ham with sautéed mushrooms or chopped cooked spinach.

Serves 2

INGREDIENTS
1 quantity Basic or Superquick Pizza
  Dough
4 oz ricotta
2 tbsp freshly grated Parmesan
1 egg yolk
2 tbsp chopped fresh basil
3 oz cooked ham, finely chopped
3 oz mozzarella, cut into small cubes
olive oil for brushing
salt and black pepper

basil

ricotta

egg

mozzarella

Parmesan

cooked ham

1 Preheat the oven to 425°F. Divide the dough in to two pieces and roll out each piece on a lightly floured surface to a 7 in circle.

2 In a bowl mix together the ricotta, Parmesan, egg yolk, basil and seasoning.

3 Spread the mixture over half of each circle, leaving a 1 in border, then scatter the ham and mozzarella on top. Dampen the edges with water, then fold over the other half of dough to enclose the filling.

4 Press the edges firmly together to seal. Place on two greased baking sheets. Brush with oil and make a small hole in the top of each to allow the steam to escape. Bake for 15–20 minutes until golden. Serve immediately.

Smoked Chicken, Yellow Pepper and Sun-dried Tomato Pizzettes

These ingredients complement each other perfectly and make a really delicious topping.

Serves 4

INGREDIENTS
1 quantity Basic or Superquick Pizza
  Dough
3 tbsp olive oil
4 tbsp sun-dried tomato paste
2 yellow bell peppers, seeded and cut
  into thin strips
6 oz sliced smoked chicken or turkey,
  chopped
5 oz mozzarella, cubed
2 tbsp chopped fresh basil
salt and black pepper

basil

mozzarella

yellow bell peppers

olive oil

smoked chicken

sun-dried tomato paste

1 Preheat the oven to 425°F. Divide the dough into four pieces and roll out each one on a lightly floured surface to a 5 in circle. Place well apart on two greased baking sheets, then pinch up the dough edges to make a thin rim. Brush with 1 tbsp of the oil.

2 Brush the pizza bases generously with the sun-dried tomato paste.

3 Stir-fry the peppers in half the remaining oil for 3–4 minutes.

4 Arrange the chicken and peppers on top of the sun-dried tomato paste.

5 Scatter the mozzarella and basil over. Season with salt and black pepper.

VARIATION

For a vegetarian pizza with a similar smoky taste, omit the chicken, roast the yellow peppers and remove the skins before using, and replace the mozzarella with Gouda smoked cheese.

6 Drizzle over the remaining oil and bake for 15–20 minutes until crisp and golden. Serve immediately.

Spicy Sausage

This is a tasty and substantial pizza. You may substitute fresh Italian spicy sausages, available from good Italian delicatessens, if you prefer.

Serves 3–4

INGREDIENTS
8 oz good quality pork sausages
1 tsp mild chili powder
½ tsp freshly ground black pepper
2 tbsp olive oil
2–3 garlic cloves
1 pizza base, about 10–12 in
   diameter
1 quantity Tomato Sauce
1 red onion, thinly sliced
1 tbsp chopped fresh oregano
1 tbsp chopped fresh thyme
2 oz mozzarella, grated
2 oz freshly grated Parmesan

Tomato Sauce

thyme and oregano

red onion

Parmesan

mozzarella

olive oil

pork sausages

mild chili powder

1 Preheat the oven to 425°F. Skin the sausages by running a sharp knife down the side of the skins. Place the sausage meat in a bowl and add the chili powder and black pepper; mix well. Break the sausage meat mixture into walnut-sized balls.

2 Heat 1 tbsp of the oil in a frying pan and fry the sausage balls for 2–3 minutes until evenly browned.

3 Using a slotted spoon remove the sausage balls from the pan and drain on paper towels.

4 Thinly slice the garlic cloves.

5 Brush the pizza base with the remaining oil, then spread over the Tomato Sauce. Scatter the sausages, garlic, onion and herbs over.

6 Sprinkle over the mozzarella and Parmesan and bake for 15–20 minutes until crisp and golden. Serve immediately.

Caramelized Onion, Salami and Black Olive

The flavor of the sweet caramelized onion is offset by the salty black olives and herbes de Provence in the pizza base and the sprinkling of Parmesan to finish.

Serves 4

INGREDIENTS
1½ lb red onions
4 tbsp olive oil
12 pitted black olives
1 quantity Basic or Superquick Pizza Dough
1 tsp dried herbes de Provence
6–8 slices Italian salami, quartered
2–3 tbsp freshly grated Parmesan
black pepper

Italian salami

olive oil

red onions

Parmesan

black olives

herbes de Provence

1 Preheat the oven to 425°F. Thinly slice the onions.

2 Heat 2 tbsp of the oil in a pan and add the onions. Cover and cook gently for 15–20 minutes, stirring occasionally until the onions are soft and very lightly colored. Leave to cool.

3 Finely chop the black olives.

4 Knead the dough on a lightly floured surface, adding the black olives and herbes de Provence. Roll out the dough and use to line a 12 × 7 in jelly roll pan. Pinch up the dough edges to make a thin rim and brush with half the remaining oil.

5 Spoon half the onions over the base, top with the salami and the remaining onions.

6 Grind over plenty of black pepper and drizzle over the remaining oil. Bake for 15–20 minutes until crisp and golden. Remove from the oven and sprinkle the Parmesan over to serve.

Ham and Pineapple French Bread Pizza

French bread makes a great pizza base. For a really speedy recipe use ready-made pizza topping instead of the Tomato Sauce.

Serves 4

INGREDIENTS
2 small baguettes
1 quantity Tomato Sauce
3 oz sliced cooked ham
4 rings canned pineapple, drained
   well and chopped
½ small green bell pepper, seeded
   and cut into thin strips
3 oz sharp Cheddar
salt and black pepper

green bell pepper

sharp Cheddar

pineapple

cooked ham

baguette

Tomato Sauce

1 Preheat the oven to 400°F. Cut the baguettes in half lengthwise and toast the cut sides until crisp and golden.

2 Spread the Tomato Sauce over the toasted baguettes.

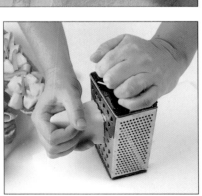

3 Cut the ham into strips and arrange on the baguettes with the pineapple and pepper. Season.

4 Grate the Cheddar and sprinkle on top. Bake or broil for 15–20 minutes until crisp and golden.

Prosciutto, Roasted Bell Peppers and Mozzarella Pizzas

Succulent roasted peppers, salty prosciutto and creamy mozzarella – the delicious flavors of these easy pizzas are hard to beat.

Serves 2

INGREDIENTS
½ loaf country bread
1 red bell pepper, roasted and peeled
1 yellow bell pepper, roasted and peeled
4 slices prosciutto, cut into thick strips
3 oz mozzarella
black pepper
tiny basil leaves, to garnish

country bread

basil

mozzarella

prosciutto

red and yellow bell peppers

1 Cut the bread into four thick slices and toast both sides until golden.

2 Cut the roasted peppers into thick strips and arrange on the toasted bread with the prosciutto.

3 Thinly slice the mozzarella and arrange on top. Grind plenty of black pepper over. Place under a hot broiler for 2–3 minutes until the cheese is bubbling.

4 Arrange the basil leaves on top and serve immediately.

Pepperoni Pan Pizza

This pizza is made using a scone base which happily does not require proving! The topping can be varied to include whatever you like best – tunafish, shrimp, ham or salami are all good alternatives to the pepperoni.

Serves 2–3

INGREDIENTS
1 tbsp chopped fresh mixed herbs
1 quantity Scone Pizza Dough
2 tbsp tomato paste
14 oz can crushed tomatoes, drained well
2 oz mushrooms, thinly sliced
3 oz sliced pepperoni
6 pitted black olives, chopped
2 oz Edam, grated
2 oz sharp Cheddar, grated
1 tbsp chopped fresh basil, to garnish

1 Add the herbs to the scone mix before mixing to a soft dough.

2 Turn the dough on to a lightly floured surface and knead lightly until smooth. Roll out to fit a well-greased frying pan, about 8½ in diameter.

3 Cook the dough in the pan over a low heat for about 5 minutes until the base is golden. Lift carefully with a spatula to check.

sharp Cheddar

Edam

mushrooms

chopped tomatoes

black olives *basil* *fresh mixed herbs*

pepperoni

  tomato paste

4 Turn the base on to a baking sheet, then slide it back into the pan, with the cooked side uppermost.

5 Mix together the tomato paste and drained tomatoes and spread over the pizza base. Scatter over the mushrooms, pepperoni, olives and cheeses. Continue to cook for about 5 minutes until the underside is golden.

6 When it is ready, transfer the pan to a preheated moderate broiler for 4–5 minutes to melt the cheese. Scatter the basil over and serve immediately.

Mixed Seafood

Here is a pizza that gives you the full flavor of the Mediterranean, ideal for a summer evening supper!

Serves 3–4

INGREDIENTS
1 pizza base, 10–12 in diameter
2 tbsp olive oil
1 quantity Tomato Sauce
14 oz mixed cooked seafood
   (including mussels, shrimp and
   squid)
3 garlic cloves
2 tbsp chopped fresh parsley
2 tbsp freshly grated Parmesan, to
   garnish

mixed seafood

garlic

olive oil

parsley

Tomato Sauce

Parmesan

1 Preheat the oven to 425°F. Brush the pizza base with 1 tbsp of the oil.

2 Spread the Tomato Sauce over. Bake in the oven for 10 minutes. Remove from the oven.

3 Pat the seafood dry using paper towels, then arrange on top.

4 Chop the garlic and sprinkle over.

5 Sprinkle the parsley over, then drizzle the remaining oil over.

VARIATION

If you prefer, this pizza can be made with mussels or shrimp on their own, or any combination of your favorite seafood.

6 Bake for a further 5–10 minutes until the seafood is warmed through and the base is crisp and golden. Sprinkle with Parmesan and serve immediately.

Salmon and Avocado

Smoked and fresh salmon make a delicious pizza topping when mixed with avocado. Smoked salmon trimmings are cheaper than smoked salmon slices and could be used instead.

Serves 3–4

INGREDIENTS

5 oz salmon fillet
½ cup dry white wine
1 pizza base, 10–12 in diameter
1 tbsp olive oil
14 oz can chopped tomatoes, drained
   well
4 oz mozzarella, grated
1 small avocado
2 tsp lemon juice
2 tbsp crème fraîche
3 oz smoked salmon, cut into
   strips
1 tbsp capers
2 tbsp chopped fresh chives, to
   garnish
black pepper

lemon

dry white wine

chopped tomatoes

mozzarella

avocado

smoked salmon

salmon fillet

crème fraîche

1 Preheat the oven to 425°F. Place the salmon fillet in a frying pan, pour the wine over and season with black pepper. Bring slowly to a boil, remove from the heat, cover and cool. (The fish will continue to cook in the cooling liquid.) Skin and flake the salmon into small pieces, removing any bones.

2 Brush the pizza base with the oil and spread over the drained tomatoes. Sprinkle 2 oz of the mozzarella over. Bake for 10 minutes, then remove from the oven.

3 Meanwhile, halve, pit and peel the avocado. Cut the flesh into small cubes and toss carefully in the lemon juice.

4 Dot teaspoonsful of the crème fraîche over the pizza base.

5 Arrange the fresh and smoked salmon, avocado, capers and remaining mozzarella on top. Season with black pepper. Bake for a further 5–10 minutes until crisp and golden.

6 Sprinkle the chives over and serve immediately.

Shrimp, Sun-dried Tomato and Basil Pizzettes

Sun-dried tomatoes with their concentrated caramelized tomato flavor make an excellent topping for pizzas. Serve these pretty pizzettes as an appetizer or snack.

Serves 4

INGREDIENTS
1 quantity Basic or Superquick Pizza
   Dough
2 tbsp Chili Oil
3 oz mozzarella, grated
1 garlic clove, chopped
½ small red onion, thinly sliced
4–6 pieces sun-dried tomatoes, thinly
   sliced
4 oz cooked shrimp, peeled
2 tbsp chopped fresh basil
salt and black pepper
shredded basil leaves, to garnish

basil

mozzarella

Chili Oil

red onion

sun-dried tomatoes

garlic

1 Preheat the oven to 425°F. Divide the dough into eight pieces.

2 Roll out each one on a lightly floured surface to a small oval about ¼ in thick. Place well apart on two greased baking sheets. Prick all over with a fork.

3 Brush the pizza bases with 1 tbsp of the chili oil and top with the mozzarella, leaving a ½ in border.

4 Divide the garlic, onion, sun-dried tomatoes, shrimp and basil between the pizza bases. Season and drizzle the remaining chili oil over. Bake for 8–10 minutes until crisp and golden. Garnish with basil leaves and serve immediately.

Crab and Parmesan Calzonelli

These miniature calzone owe their popularity to their impressive presentation. If preferred, you can use shrimp instead of crab.

Makes 10–12

INGREDIENTS
1 quantity Basic or Superquick Pizza
   Dough
4 oz mixed prepared crabmeat,
   defrosted if frozen
1 tbsp heavy cream
2 tbsp freshly grated Parmesan
2 tbsp chopped fresh parsley
1 garlic clove, crushed
salt and black pepper
parsley sprigs, to garnish

Parmesan

heavy cream

crabmeat

parsley

garlic

1 Preheat the oven to 400°F. Roll out the dough on a lightly floured surface to ⅛ in thick. Using a 3 in plain round cutter stamp out 10–12 circles.

2 In a bowl mix together the crabmeat, cream, Parmesan, parsley, garlic and seasoning.

3 Spoon a little of the filling on to one half of each circle. Dampen the edges with water and fold over to enclose filling.

4 Seal the edges by pressing with a fork. Place well apart on two greased baking sheets. Bake for 10–15 minutes until golden. Garnish with parsley sprigs.

Mussel and Leek Pizzettes

Serve these tasty seafood pizzettes with a crisp green
salad for a light lunch.

Serves 4

INGREDIENTS
1 lb live mussels
½ cup dry white wine
1 quantity Basic or Superquick Pizza
   Dough
1 tbsp olive oil
2 oz Gruyère
2 oz mozzarella
2 small leeks
salt and black pepper

olive oil

dry white wine

mozzarella

mussels

Gruyère

leeks

1 Preheat the oven to 425°F. Place the
mussels in a bowl of cold water to soak,
and scrub well. Remove the beards and
discard any mussels that are open.

2 Place the mussels in a pan. Pour over
the wine, cover and cook over a high
heat, shaking the pan occasionally, for
5–10 minutes until the mussels have
opened.

3 Drain off the cooking liquid. Remove
the mussels from their shells, discarding
any that remain closed. Leave to cool.

4 Divide the dough into four pieces
and roll out each one on a lightly floured
surface to a 5 in circle. Place well apart on
two greased baking sheets, then pinch up
the dough edges to form a thin rim. Brush
the pizza bases with the oil. Grate the
cheeses and sprinkle half evenly over the
bases.

5 Thinly slice the leeks, then scatter over the cheese. Bake for 10 minutes, then
remove from the oven.

VARIATION

Frozen or canned mussels can also be used, but will not have the same flavor and texture. Make sure you defrost the mussels properly.

6 Arrange the mussels on top. Season and sprinkle the remaining cheese over. Bake for a further 5–10 minutes until crisp and golden. Serve immediately.

Anchovy, Pepper and Tomato

This pretty, summery pizza is utterly simple, yet quite delicious. It's well worth broiling the peppers as they take on a subtle smoky flavor.

Serves 2–3

INGREDIENTS
6 plum tomatoes
3 tbsp olive oil
1 tsp salt
1 large red bell pepper
1 large yellow bell pepper
1 pizza base, 10–12 in diameter
2 garlic cloves, chopped
2 oz can anchovy fillets, drained
 and chopped
black pepper
basil leaves, to garnish

olive oil

*red and yellow
bell peppers*

plum tomatoes

garlic

anchovy fillets

1 Halve the tomatoes lengthwise and scoop out the seeds.

2 Coarsely chop the flesh and place in a bowl with 1 tbsp of the oil and the salt. Mix well, then leave to marinate for 30 minutes.

3 Meanwhile, preheat the oven to 425°F. Slice the peppers in half lengthwise and remove the seeds. Place the pepper halves, skin-side up, on a baking sheet and broil until the skins of the peppers are evenly charred.

4 Place the peppers in a covered bowl for 10 minutes, then peel off the skins. Cut the flesh into thin strips.

5 Brush the pizza base with half the remaining oil. Drain the tomatoes, then scatter over the base with the peppers and garlic.

6 Sprinkle on the anchovy fillets and season with black pepper. Drizzle over the remaining oil and bake for 15–20 minutes until crisp and golden. Garnish with basil leaves and serve immediately.

Tuna, Anchovy and Caper

This pizza makes a substantial supper dish which will provide two to three generous portions accompanied by a simple salad.

Serves 2–3

INGREDIENTS
1 quantity Scone Pizza Dough
30 ml/2 tbsp olive oil
1 quantity Tomato Sauce
1 small red onion
200 g/7 oz can tuna, drained
15 ml/1 tbsp capers
12 pitted black olives
45 ml/3 tbsp freshly grated Parmesan
50 g/2 oz can anchovy fillets, drained and halved lengthways
black pepper

Tomato Sauce

olive oil

Parmesan

black olives

tuna

red onion

capers

1 Preheat the oven to 425°F. Roll out the dough on a lightly floured surface to a 10 in circle. Place on a greased baking sheet and brush with 1 tbsp of the oil. Spread the Tomato Sauce evenly over the dough.

2 Cut the onion into thin wedges and arrange on top.

3 Coarsely flake the tuna with a fork and scatter the onion over.

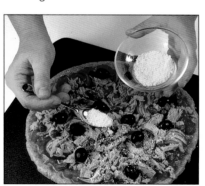

4 Sprinkle the capers, black olives and Parmesan over.

5 Lattice the anchovy fillets over the top of the pizza.

6 Drizzle the remaining oil over, then grind over plenty of black pepper. Bake for 15–20 minutes until crisp and golden. Serve immediately.

Roasted Vegetable and Goat Cheese

Here is a pizza which incorporates the smoky flavors of oven-roasted vegetables with the distinctive taste of goat cheese.

Serves 3

INGREDIENTS
1 eggplant, cut into thick chunks
2 small zucchini, sliced lengthwise
1 red bell pepper, quartered and
  seeded
1 yellow bell pepper, quartered and
  seeded
1 small red onion, cut into wedges
6 tbsp Garlic Oil
1 pizza base, 10–12 in diameter
1 × 14 oz can chopped tomatoes,
  drained well
1 × 4 oz goat cheese (with rind)
1 tbsp chopped fresh thyme
black pepper
green olive tapenade, to serve

1 Preheat the oven to 425°F. Place the eggplant, zucchini, peppers and onion in a large roasting pan. Brush with 4 tbsp of the Garlic Oil. Roast for about 30 minutes until lightly charred, turning the peppers halfway through cooking. Remove from the oven and set aside.

2 When the peppers are cool enough to handle, peel off the skins and cut the flesh into thick strips.

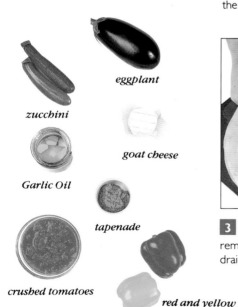

eggplant

zucchini

goat cheese

Garlic Oil

tapenade

crushed tomatoes

red and yellow bell peppers

3 Brush the pizza base with half the remaining Garlic Oil and spread over the drained tomatoes.

4 Arrange the roasted vegetables on top of the pizza.

5 Cube the goat cheese and arrange on top. Scatter the thyme over.

COOK'S TIP

If you place the roasted peppers in a paper bag while they cool, peeling off the skins becomes easier.

6 Drizzle the remaining Garlic Oil over and season with black pepper. Bake for 15–20 minutes until crisp and golden. Spoon the tapenade over to serve.

New Potato, Rosemary and Garlic

New potatoes, smoked mozzarella, rosemary and garlic make the flavor of this pizza unique. For a delicious variation, use sage instead of rosemary.

Serves 2–3

INGREDIENTS
12 oz new potatoes
3 tbsp olive oil
2 garlic cloves, crushed
1 pizza base, 10–12 in diameter
1 red onion, thinly sliced
5 oz smoked mozzarella, grated
2 tsp chopped fresh rosemary
salt and black pepper
2 tbsp freshly grated Parmesan, to
    garnish

olive oil

Parmesan

smoked mozzarella

new potatoes

rosemary

red onion

garlic

1 Preheat the oven to 425°F. Cook the potatoes in boiling salted water for 5 minutes. Drain well. When cool, peel and slice thinly.

2 Heat 2 tbsp of the oil in a frying pan. Add the sliced potatoes and garlic and fry for 5–8 minutes until tender.

3 Brush the pizza base with the remaining oil. Scatter the onion over, then arrange the potatoes on top.

4 Sprinkle over the mozzarella and rosemary. Grind over plenty of black pepper and bake for 15–20 minutes until crisp and golden. Remove from the oven and sprinkle the Parmesan over to serve.

Wild Mushroom Pizzettes

Serve these extravagant pizzas as a starter. Fresh wild mushrooms add a distinctive flavor to the topping but a mixture of cultivated mushrooms such as shiitake, oyster and cremini mushrooms would do just as well.

Serves 4

INGREDIENTS
3 tbsp olive oil
12 oz fresh wild mushrooms, washed
   and sliced
2 shallots, chopped
2 garlic cloves, finely chopped
2 tbsp chopped fresh mixed thyme
   and Italian parsley
1 quantity Basic or Superquick Pizza
   Dough
1½ oz Gruyère, grated
2 tbsp freshly grated Parmesan
salt and black pepper

Gruyère

Italian parsley

thyme

olive oil

Parmesan

garlic
shallots

wild mushrooms

1 Preheat the oven to 425°F. Heat 2 tbsp of the oil in a frying pan. Add the mushrooms, shallots and garlic and fry over a moderate heat until all the juices have evaporated.

2 Stir in half the herbs and seasoning, then set aside to cool.

3 Divide the dough into four pieces and roll out each one on a lightly floured surface to a 5 in circle. Place well apart on two greased baking sheets, then pinch up the dough edges to form a thin rim. Brush the pizza bases with the remaining oil and top with the wild mushroom mixture.

4 Mix together the Gruyère and Parmesan, then sprinkle over. Bake for 15–20 minutes until crisp and golden. Remove from the oven and sprinkle the remaining herbs over to serve.

Chili, Tomatoes and Spinach

This richly flavored topping with a hint of spice makes a colorful and satisfying pizza.

Serves 3

INGREDIENTS
1–2 fresh red chilies
3 tbsp tomato oil (from jar of sun-
   dried tomatoes)
1 onion, chopped
2 garlic cloves, chopped
2 oz (drained weight) sun-dried
   tomatoes in oil
14 oz can crushed tomatoes
1 tbsp tomato paste
6 oz fresh spinach
1 pizza base, 10–12 in diameter
3 oz smoked Gouda cheese, grated
3 oz sharp Cheddar, grated
salt and black pepper

1 Seed and finely chop the chilies.

2 Heat 2 tbsp of the tomato oil in a pan, add the onion, garlic and chilies and gently fry for about 5 minutes until they are soft.

3 Coarsely chop the sun-dried tomatoes. Add to the pan with the crushed tomatoes, tomato paste and seasoning. Simmer uncovered, stirring occasionally, for 15 minutes.

smoked Gouda cheese

crushed tomatoes

sharp Cheddar

sun-dried tomatoes

onion

garlic

spinach

red chilies

tomato oil

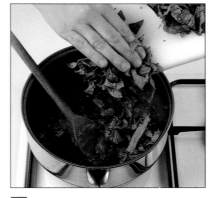

4 Remove the stems from the spinach and wash the leaves in plenty of cold water. Drain well and pat dry with paper towels. Coarsely chop the spinach.

5 Stir the spinach into the sauce. Cook, stirring, for a further 5–10 minutes until the spinach has wilted and no excess moisture remains. Leave to cool.

6 Meanwhile, preheat the oven to 425°F. Brush the pizza base with the remaining tomato oil, then spoon the sauce over. Sprinkle the cheeses over and bake for 15–20 minutes until crisp and golden. Serve immediately.

Tomato, Pesto and Black Olive

These individual pizzas take very little time to put together. Marinating the tomatoes gives them extra flavor.

Serves 4

INGREDIENTS
2 plum tomatoes
1 garlic clove, crushed
4 tbsp olive oil
1 quantity Basic or Superquick Pizza
    Dough
2 tbsp red pesto
5 oz mozzarella, thinly sliced
4 pitted black olives, chopped
1 tbsp chopped fresh oregano
salt and black pepper
oregano leaves, to garnish

red pesto

mozzarella

oregano

plum tomatoes

black olives

1 Slice the tomatoes thinly crosswise, then cut each slice in half. Place the tomatoes in a shallow dish with the garlic. Drizzle 2 tbsp of the oil over and season. Let marinate for 15 minutes.

2 Meanwhile, preheat the oven to 425°F. Divide the dough into four pieces and roll out each one on a lightly floured surface to a 5 in circle. Place well apart on two greased baking sheets, then pinch up the dough edges to make a rim. Brush the pizza bases with half the remaining oil and spread over the pesto.

3 Drain the tomatoes, then arrange a fan of alternate slices of tomatoes and mozzarella on each base.

4 Sprinkle over the olives and oregano. Drizzle over the remaining oil on top and bake for 15–20 minutes until crisp and golden. Garnish with the oregano leaves and serve immediately.

Fresh Herb

Cut this pizza into thin wedges and serve as part of a mixed antipasti.

Serves 8

INGREDIENTS
4 oz mixed fresh herbs, such as
  parsley, basil and oregano
3 garlic cloves, crushed
½ cup heavy cream
1 pizza base, 10–12 in diameter
1 tbsp Garlic Oil
4 oz Pecorino, grated
salt and black pepper

heavy cream

Garlic Oil

Pecorino

basil

parsley

garlic

1 Preheat the oven to 425°F. Chop the herbs in a food processor if you have one.

2 In a bowl mix together the herbs, garlic, cream and seasoning.

3 Brush the pizza base with the Garlic Oil, then spread the herb mixture over.

4 Sprinkle the Pecorino over. Bake for 15–20 minutes until crisp and golden and the topping is still moist. Cut into thin wedges and serve immediately.

Eggplant, Shallot and Sun-dried Tomato Calzone

Eggplant, shallots and sun-dried tomatoes make an unusual filling for calzone. Add more or less red chili flakes, depending on personal taste.

Serves 2

INGREDIENTS
3 tbsp olive oil
3 shallots, chopped
4 baby eggplants
1 garlic clove, chopped
2 oz (drained weight) sun-dried
   tomatoes in oil, chopped
¼ tsp dried red chilli flakes
2 tsp chopped fresh thyme
1 quantity Basic or Superquick Pizza
   Dough
3 oz mozzarella, cubed
salt and black pepper
1–2 tbsp freshly grated Parmesan, to
   serve

Parmesan

thyme

mozzarella

olive oil

baby eggplants

shallots

red chili flakes

1 Preheat the oven to 425°F. Heat 2 tbsp of the oil in a frying pan. Add the shallots and cook until soft. Trim the eggplants, then cut into small cubes.

2 Add the eggplants to the shallots with the garlic, sun-dried tomatoes, red chili flakes, thyme and seasoning. Cook for 4–5 minutes, stirring frequently, until the eggplant is beginning to soften. Remove from the heat and let cool.

3 Divide the dough in half and roll out each piece on a lightly floured surface to a 7 in circle.

4 Spread the eggplant mixture over half of each circle, leaving a 1 in border, then scatter the mozzarella over.

5 Dampen the edges with water, then fold over the other half of dough to enclose the filling. Press the edges firmly together to seal. Place on two greased baking sheets.

6 Brush with half the remaining oil and make a small hole in the top of each to allow the steam to escape. Bake for 15–20 minutes until golden. Remove from the oven and brush with the remaining oil. Sprinkle the Parmesan over and serve immediately.

Tomato, Fennel and Parmesan

This pizza relies on the winning combination of tomatoes, fennel and Parmesan. The fennel adds both a crisp texture and a distinctive flavor.

Serves 2–3

INGREDIENTS
1 fennel bulb
3 tbsp Garlic Oil
1 pizza base, 10–12 in diameter
1 quantity Tomato Sauce
2 tbsp chopped fresh Italian parsley
2 oz mozzarella, grated
2 oz Parmesan, grated
salt and black pepper

Italian parsley

mozzarella

Tomato Sauce

Parmesan

fennel bulb

Garlic Oil

1 Preheat the oven to 425°F. Trim and quarter the fennel lengthwise. Remove the core and slice each quarter of fennel thinly.

2 Heat 2 tbsp of the Garlic Oil in a frying pan and sauté the fennel for 4–5 minutes until just tender. Season.

3 Brush the pizza base with the remaining Garlic Oil and spread over the Tomato Sauce. Spoon the fennel on top and scatter the Italian parsley over.

4 Mix together the mozzarella and Parmesan and sprinkle over. Bake for 15–20 minutes until crisp and golden. Serve immediately.

Red Onion, Gorgonzola and Sage

This topping combines the richness of Gorgonzola with the earthy flavors of sage and sweet red onions.

Serves 4

INGREDIENTS
1 quantity Basic or Superquick Pizza
   Dough
2 tbsp Garlic Oil
2 small red onions
5 oz Gorgonzola
2 garlic cloves
2 tsp chopped fresh sage
black pepper

sage

garlic

Gorgonzola

Garlic Oil

red onions

1 Preheat the oven to 425°F. Divide the dough into eight pieces and roll out each one on a lightly floured surface to a small oval about ¼ in thick. Place well apart on two greased baking sheets and prick with a fork. Brush the bases of each oval well with 1 tbsp of the Garlic Oil.

2 Halve, then slice the onions into thin wedges. Scatter over the pizza bases.

3 Remove the rind from the Gorgonzola. Cut the cheese into small cubes, then scatter it over the onions.

4 Cut the garlic lengthwise into thin strips and sprinkle over, along with the sage. Drizzle the remaining oil on top and grind over plenty of black pepper. Bake for 10–15 minutes until crisp and golden. Serve immediately.

Onion and Three Cheese

You can use any combination of cheese you like. Edam and Cheddar both have good flavors and melting properties.

Serves 3–4

INGREDIENTS
3 tbsp olive oil
3 medium onions, sliced
1 pizza base, 10–12 in diameter
4 small tomatoes, peeled, seeded and
   cut into thin wedges
2 tbsp chopped fresh basil
4 oz Saga Blue
5 oz mozzarella
4 oz Red Leicester
black pepper
fresh basil leaves, to garnish

tomatoes

mozzarella

basil

Saga Blue

Red Leicester

olive oil

onions

1 Preheat the oven to 425°F. Heat 2 tbsp of the oil in a frying pan, add the onions and gently fry for about 10 minutes, stirring occasionally. Remove from the heat and let cool.

2 Brush the pizza base with the remaining oil. Spoon the onions and tomatoes over, then scatter the basil leaves over.

3 Thinly slice the cheeses and arrange over the tomatoes and onions.

4 Grind over plenty of black pepper and bake for 15–20 minutes until crisp and golden. Garnish with basil leaves and serve immediately.

Feta, Roasted Garlic and Oregano

This is a pizza for garlic lovers! Mash down the cloves as you eat – they should be soft and will have lost their pungency.

Serves 4

INGREDIENTS
1 medium garlic head, unpeeled
3 tbsp olive oil
1 medium red bell pepper, quartered and seeded
1 medium yellow bell pepper, quartered and seeded
2 plum tomatoes
1 quantity Basic or Superquick Pizza Dough
6 oz feta, crumbled
black pepper
1–2 tbsp chopped fresh oregano, to garnish

oregano

feta

plum tomatoes

olive oil

red and yellow bell peppers

garlic head

1 Preheat the oven to 425°F. Break the head of garlic into cloves, discarding the outer papery layers. Toss in 1 tbsp of the oil.

2 Place the peppers skin-side up on a baking sheet and broil until the skins are evenly charred. Place in a covered bowl for 10 minutes, then peel off the skins. Cut the flesh into strips.

3 Put the tomatoes in a bowl and pour boiling water over. Leave for 30 seconds, then plunge into cold water. Peel, seed and coarsely chop the flesh. Divide the dough into four pieces and roll out each one on a lightly floured surface to a 5 in circle.

4 Place the dough circles well apart on two greased baking sheets, then pinch up the dough edges to form a thin rim. Brush with half the remaining oil and scatter the chopped tomatoes over. Top with the peppers, crumbled feta and garlic cloves. Drizzle over the remaining oil and season with black pepper. Bake for 15–20 minutes until crisp and golden. Garnish with chopped oregano and serve immediately.

Spring Vegetable and Pine Nuts

This colorful pizza is well worth the time it takes to prepare. You can vary the ingredients according to availability.

Serves 2–3

INGREDIENTS
1 pizza base, 10–12 in diameter
3 tbsp Garlic Oil
1 quantity Tomato Sauce
4 scallions
2 zucchini
1 leek
4 oz asparagus tips
1 tbsp chopped fresh oregano
2 tbsp pine nuts
2 oz mozzarella, grated
2 tbsp freshly grated Parmesan
black pepper

Parmesan

mozzarella

Tomato Sauce

scallions

leek

zucchini

asparagus

pine nuts

1 Preheat the oven to 425°F. Brush the pizza base with 1 tbsp of the Garlic Oil, then spread the Tomato Sauce over.

2 Slice the scallions, zucchini, leek and asparagus.

3 Heat half the remaining Garlic Oil in a frying pan and stir-fry the vegetables for 3–5 minutes.

4 Arrange the vegetables over the Tomato Sauce.

5 Sprinkle the oregano and pine nuts over the pizza.

6 Mix together the mozzarella and Parmesan and sprinkle over. Drizzle the remaining Garlic Oil over and season with black pepper. Bake for 15–20 minutes until crisp and golden. Serve immediately.

PARTY PIZZAS

Spinach and Ricotta Panzerotti

These make great party food to serve with drinks or as tasty appetizers for a crowd.

Makes 20–24

INGREDIENTS
4 oz frozen chopped spinach, defrosted and squeezed dry
2 oz ricotta
2 oz freshly grated Parmesan
generous pinch freshly grated nutmeg
2 quantities Basic or Superquick Pizza Dough
1 egg white, lightly beaten
vegetable oil for deep-frying
salt and black pepper

nutmeg

ricotta

vegetable oil

egg

frozen spinach

Parmesan

1 Place the spinach, ricotta, Parmesan, nutmeg and seasoning in a bowl and beat until smooth.

2 Roll out the dough on a lightly floured surface to about ⅛ in thick. Using a 3 in plain round cutter stamp out 20–24 circles.

3 Spread a teaspoon of spinach mixture over one half of each circle.

4 Brush the edges of the dough with a little egg white.

5 Fold the dough over the filling and press the edges firmly together to seal.

COOK'S TIP

Do serve these as soon as possible after frying, they will become much less appetizing if left to cool.

6 Heat the oil in a large heavy-based pan or deep-fat fryer to 350°F. Deep-fry the panzerotti a few at a time for 2–3 minutes until golden. Drain on paper towels and serve immediately.

Smoked Salmon Pizzettes

Mini pizzas topped with smoked salmon, crème fraîche and lumpfish caviar make an extra special party canapé.

Makes 10–12

INGREDIENTS
1 quantity Basic or Superquick Pizza
    Dough
1 tbsp chopped fresh chives
1 tbsp olive oil
3–4 oz smoked salmon, cut into strips
4 tbsp crème fraîche
2 tbsp black lumpfish caviar
chives, to garnish

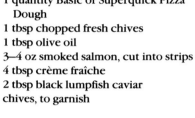

crème fraîche

olive oil

smoked salmon

chives

black lumpfish caviar

1 Preheat the oven to 400°F. Knead the dough gently, adding the chives until evenly mixed.

2 Roll out the dough on a lightly floured surface to about ⅛ in thick. Using a 3 in plain round cutter stamp out 10–12 circles.

3 Place the bases well apart on two greased baking sheets, prick all over with a fork, then brush with the oil. Bake for 10–15 minutes until crisp and golden.

4 Arrange the smoked salmon on top, then spoon on the crème fraîche. Spoon a tiny amount of lumpfish caviar in the center and garnish with chives. Serve immediately.

Sun-dried Tomatoes, Basil and Olive Pizza Bites

This quick and easy recipe uses scone pizza dough with the addition of chopped fresh basil.

Makes 24

INGREDIENTS
18–20 fresh basil leaves
1 quantity Scone Pizza Dough
2 tbsp tomato oil (from jar of sun-dried tomatoes)
1 quantity Tomato Sauce
4 oz (drained weight) sun-dried tomatoes in oil, chopped
10 pitted black olives, chopped
2 oz mozzarella, grated
2 tbsp freshly grated Parmesan
shredded basil leaves, to garnish

black olives

mozzarella

Parmesan

Tomato Sauce

tomato oil

basil

sun-dried tomatoes

1 Preheat the oven to 425°F. Tear the basil leaves into small pieces. Add half to the scone mix before mixing to a soft dough. Set aside the remainder.

2 Knead the dough gently on a lightly floured surface until smooth. Roll out and use to line a 12 × 7 in jelly roll pan. Pinch up the edges to make a thin rim.

3 Brush the base with 1 tbsp of the tomato oil, then spread the Tomato Sauce over. Scatter the sun-dried tomatoes, olives and remaining basil over.

4 Mix together the mozzarella and Parmesan and sprinkle over. Drizzle the remaining tomato oil over. Bake for about 20 minutes. Cut lengthwise and across into 24 bite-size pieces. Garnish with extra shredded basil leaves and serve immediately.

Farmhouse Pizza

This is the ultimate party pizza. Served cut into fingers, it is ideal for a crowd.

Serves 8

INGREDIENTS
6 tbsp olive oil
8 oz mushrooms, sliced
2 quantities Basic or Superquick Pizza
    Dough
1 quantity Tomato Sauce
10 oz mozzarella, thinly sliced
4 oz paper-thin smoked ham slices
6 bottled artichoke hearts in oil,
    drained and sliced
2 oz can anchovy fillets, drained and
    halved lengthwise
10 pitted black olives, halved
2 tbsp chopped fresh oregano
3 tbsp freshly grated Parmesan
black pepper

anchovy fillets

mozzarella

artichoke hearts

smoked ham

olive oil

Tomato Sauce

black olives

mushrooms

1 Preheat the oven to 425°F. Heat 2 tbsp of the oil in a large frying pan, add the mushrooms and fry for about 5 minutes until all the juices have evaporated. Leave to cool.

2 Roll out the dough on a lightly floured surface to a 12 × 10 in rectangle. Transfer to a greased baking sheet, then pinch up the dough edges to make a thin rim. Brush the dough with 2 tbsp of the oil.

3 Spread the Tomato Sauce over.

4 Arrange the sliced mozzarella over the sauce.

5 Scrunch up the ham and arrange on top with the artichoke hearts, mushrooms and anchovies.

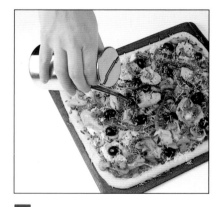

6 Dot with the olives, then sprinkle the oregano and Parmesan over. Drizzle over the remaining oil and season with black pepper. Bake for about 25 minutes until crisp and golden. Serve immediately.

Feta, Pimiento and Pine Nut

Delight your guests with these tempting pizzas.
Substitute goat cheese for the feta if you prefer.

Makes 24

INGREDIENTS
2 quantities Basic or Superquick Pizza
  Dough
4 tbsp olive oil
2 tbsp black olive tapenade
6 oz feta
1 large canned pimiento, drained
2 tbsp chopped fresh thyme
2 tbsp pine nuts
black pepper
thyme sprigs, to garnish

pimiento

thyme

feta cheese

tapenade

pine nuts

1 Preheat the oven to 425°F. Divide the dough into 24 pieces and roll out each one on a lightly floured surface to a small oval, about ⅛ in thick. Place the ovals, well apart, on greased baking sheets and prick all over with a fork. Brush each one with 2 tbsp of the oil.

2 Spread a thin layer of the black olive tapenade on each oval and crumble the feta over.

3 Cut the pimiento into thin strips and pile on top.

4 Sprinkle each one with thyme and pine nuts. Drizzle the remaining oil over and grind over plenty of black pepper. Bake for 10–15 minutes until crisp and golden. Garnish with thyme sprigs and serve immediately.

Mozzarella, Anchovy and Pesto

These unusual pizzas combine the piquancy of olives and capers with anchovies and mozzarella.

Makes 24

INGREDIENTS
2 ready-to-cook pizza bases, about
    8 in diameter
4 tbsp olive oil
2 tbsp red pesto
12 stoned black olives
3 oz mozzarella, cubed
2 oz (drained weight) sun-dried
    tomatoes in oil, chopped
30–45/2–3 tbsp capers
2 oz can anchovy fillets, drained and
    coarsely chopped
2 tbsp freshly grated Parmesan
parsley sprigs, to garnish

sun-dried tomatoes

parsley

capers

mozzarella

black olives

olive oil

red pesto

anchovy fillets

1 Preheat the oven to 425°F. Using a 2 in plain round cutter stamp out 24 rounds from the pizza bases. Place the rounds on two greased baking sheets.

2 Brush the bases with 2 tbsp of the oil, then spread the pesto over.

3 Cut the olives into quarters lengthwise, then scatter over the bases with the mozzarella, sun-dried tomatoes, capers and anchovies.

4 Sprinkle over the Parmesan and drizzle the remaining oil over. Bake for 8–10 minutes until crisp and golden. Garnish with parsley sprigs and serve immediately.

Sun-dried Tomato Bread

This savory bread tastes delicious on its own, but it also makes exceptional sandwiches.

Makes 1 loaf

INGREDIENTS
3¼ cups bread flour
1 tsp salt
2 tsp rapid-rise dried yeast
2 oz (drained weight) sun-dried
    tomatoes in oil, chopped
¾ cup lukewarm water
5 tbsp lukewarm olive oil, plus extra
    for brushing
plain flour for dusting

water

flour

olive oil

rapid-rise yeast

sun-dried tomatoes

salt

1 Sift the flour and salt into a large mixing bowl.

2 Stir in the yeast and sun-dried tomatoes.

3 Make a well in the center of the dry ingredients. Pour in the water and oil, and mix until the ingredients come together and form a soft dough.

4 Turn the dough on to a lightly floured surface and knead for about 10 minutes.

5 Shape into an oblong loaf, without making the top too smooth, and place on a greased baking sheet. Brush the top with oil, cover with plastic wrap, then let rise in a warm place for about 1 hour.

6 Meanwhile, preheat the oven to 425°F. Remove the plastic wrap, then sprinkle the top of the loaf lightly with flour. Bake for 30–40 minutes until the loaf sounds hollow when tapped on the bottom. Serve warm.

Rosemary and Sea Salt Focaccia

Focaccia is an Italian flat bread made with olive oil. Here it is given added flavor with rosemary and coarse sea salt.

Makes 1 loaf

INGREDIENTS
3 cups unbleached all-purpose
    flour
½ tsp salt
2 tsp rapid-rise dried yeast
1 cup lukewarm water
3 tbsp olive oil
1 small red onion
leaves from 1 large rosemary sprig
1 tsp coarse sea salt

coarse sea salt

water

olive oil

flour

rapid-rise yeast

red onion

rosemary

1 Sift the flour and salt into a large mixing bowl. Stir in the yeast, then make a well in the center of the dry ingredients. Pour in the water and 2 tbsp of the oil. Mix well, adding a little more water if the mixture seems dry.

2 Turn the dough on to a lightly floured surface and knead for about 10 minutes until smooth and elastic.

3 Place the dough in a greased bowl, cover and let rise in a warm place for about 1 hour until doubled in size. Punch down and knead the dough for 2–3 minutes.

4 Meanwhile, preheat the oven to 425°F. Roll out the dough to a large circle, about ½ in thick, and transfer to a greased baking sheet. Brush with the remaining oil.

5 Halve the onion and slice into thin wedges. Sprinkle over the dough with the rosemary and sea salt, pressing in lightly.

6 Using a finger make deep indentations in the dough. Cover the surface with greased plastic wrap, then let rise in a warm place for 30 minutes. Remove the plastic wrap and bake for 25–30 minutes until golden. Serve warm.

Mini Focaccia with Pine Nuts

Pine nuts add little bites of nutty texture to these mini focaccias.

Makes 4 mini loaves

INGREDIENTS
3 cups unbleached all-purpose
  flour
½ tsp salt
2 tsp rapid-rise dried yeast
1 cup lukewarm water
3 tbsp olive oil
3—4 tbsp pine nuts
2 tsp coarse sea salt

water

sea salt

olive oil

flour

rapid-rise yeast

pine nuts

1 Sift the flour and salt into a large mixing bowl. Stir in the yeast, then make a well in the center of the dry ingredients. Pour in the water and 2 tbsp of the oil. Mix well, adding more water if the mixture seems dry. Turn on to a lightly floured surface and knead for about 10 minutes until smooth and elastic. Place the dough in a greased bowl, cover and let rise in a warm place for about 1 hour until doubled in size. Punch down and knead the dough for 2–3 minutes.

2 Divide the dough into four pieces.

3 Using your hands pat out each piece on greased baking sheets to a 4 × 3 in oblong, rounded at the ends.

4 Scatter the pine nuts over and gently press them into the surface. Sprinkle with salt and brush with the remaining oil. Cover with greased plastic wrap and let rise for about 30 minutes. Meanwhile, preheat the oven to 425°F. Remove the plastic wrap and bake the focaccias for 15–20 minutes until golden. Serve warm.

Walnut Bread

The nutty flavor of this wonderfully textured bread is excellent. Try it toasted and topped with melting goat cheese for a mouthwatering snack.

Makes 2 loaves

INGREDIENTS
4 cups bread flour
2 tsp salt
2 tsp rapid-rise dried yeast
1¼ cups chopped walnuts
4 tbsp chopped fresh parsley
1⅔ cups lukewarm water
4 tbsp olive oil

flour

olive oil

rapid-rise yeast

parsley

walnuts

salt

1 Sift the flour and salt into a large mixing bowl. Stir in the yeast, walnuts and parsley.

2 Make a well in the center of the dry ingredients. Pour in the water and oil and mix to a soft dough. Turn the dough on to a lightly floured surface and knead for about 10 minutes until smooth and elastic. Place in a greased bowl, cover and let rise in a warm place for about 1 hour until doubled in size.

3 Punch down and knead the dough for 2–3 minutes. Divide in half and shape each piece into a thick roll about 7–8 in long. Place on greased baking sheets, cover with plastic wrap and let rise for about 30 minutes.

4 Meanwhile, preheat the oven to 425°F. Remove the plastic wrap, then lightly slash the top of each loaf. Bake for 10 minutes, then reduce the oven temperature to 350°F. and bake for a further 25–30 minutes until the loaves sound hollow when tapped. Serve warm.

Olive Bread

Green olives are added to heighten the flavor of this moist bread. Use a combination of green and black olives if you prefer.

Makes 2 loaves

INGREDIENTS
6 cups bread flour
1 tsp salt
sachet of rapid-rise dried yeast
1 tbsp chopped fresh oregano
1½ cups lukewarm water
7 tbsp olive oil
about 30 stoned green olives

green olives

flour

oregano

rapid-rise yeast

olive oil

salt

1 Sift the flour and salt into a large mixing bowl. Stir in the yeast and oregano.

2 Measure the water into a bowl, then stir in 6 tbsp of the oil. Make a well in the center of the dry ingredients, pour in the liquid and mix to a soft dough.

3 Turn the dough on to a lightly floured surface and knead for about 10 minutes until smooth and elastic. Place in a greased bowl, cover with plastic wrap and let rise in a warm place for about 1 hour until doubled in size.

4 Punch down and knead the dough for 2–3 minutes. Divide in half, then press the dough on greased baking sheets into two ovals, about ½ in thick.

5 Using a clean finger make about 15 deep indentations over the surface of each loaf. Press an olive into each indentation.

6 Brush the loaves with the remaining oil, cover with plastic wrap and let rise for 30 minutes. Meanwhile, preheat the oven to 425°F. Remove the plastic wrap and bake for 20–25 minutes until the loaves sound hollow when tapped. Serve warm.

Saffron and Basil Breadsticks

Saffron lends its delicate aroma and flavor, as well as rich yellow color, to these tasty breadsticks.

Makes 32

INGREDIENTS
generous pinch saffron strands
4 cups bread flour
1 tsp salt
2 tsp rapid-rise dried yeast
1¼ cups lukewarm water
3 tbsp olive oil
3 tbsp chopped fresh basil

flour

water

olive oil

basil

rapid-rise yeast

saffron strands

salt

1 Infuse the saffron strands in 2 tbsp hot water for 10 minutes.

2 Sift the flour and salt into a large mixing bowl. Stir in the yeast, then make a well in the center of the dry ingredients. Pour in the water and saffron liquid and start to mix a little.

3 Add the oil and basil and continue to mix to a soft dough.

4 Turn out and knead the dough on a lightly floured surface for about 10 minutes until smooth and elastic. Place in a greased bowl, cover with plastic wrap and let rise for about 1 hour until it has doubled in size.

5 Punch down and knead the dough on a lightly floured surface for 2–3 minutes.

6 Preheat the oven to 425°F. Divide the dough into 32 pieces and shape into long sticks. Place well apart on greased baking sheets, then let rise for a further 15–30 minutes until they become puffy. Bake for about 15 minutes until crisp and golden. Serve warm.

INDEX